GUESS WHO DIDN'T TAKE A NAP?

To some of my unpaid help—Erin, Niki, Jordan, Lindsay, Jake, Ben, Tracy, Leslie, Kristin, and Carrie—with much love and many thanks.

—J.S.

Drawn with love for my little muses, Taylor and Caitlin, and Sukey—thank you. Dedicated to my Grandma and Grandpa Morton.

—R.K.

A **BABY BLUES**® COLLECTION

GUESS WHO DIDN'T TAKE A NAP?

BY

RICK KIRKMAN AND **JERRY SCOTT**

Andrews and McMeel
A Universal Press Syndicate Company
Kansas City

ISBN: 0-8362-1715-2

Library of Congress Catalog Card Number: 92-75353

First Printing, March 1993
Sixth Printing, April 1996

A MUSING

By Darryl and Wanda

WHEN I THINK OF THINGS
WE DO WITHOUT
LIKE PARTIES, TRIPS AND
DINING OUT,

FURNITURE THAT GOES
TOGETHER,
VACATION HOMES IN
SUNNY WEATHER,

LIKE MOONLIT WALKS—
JUST YOU AND ME
(NOT TO MENTION
SPONTANEITY!)

IT GETS ME DOWN UNTIL
I HEAR
THAT LITTLE CRY FROM
ONE SO DEAR,

WAAA!

REMINDING US WE'RE
NEEDED NOW
TO KISS AND SOOTHE
A FURROWED BROW.

BABY BLUES®

RICK KIRKMAN / JERRY SCOTT BY

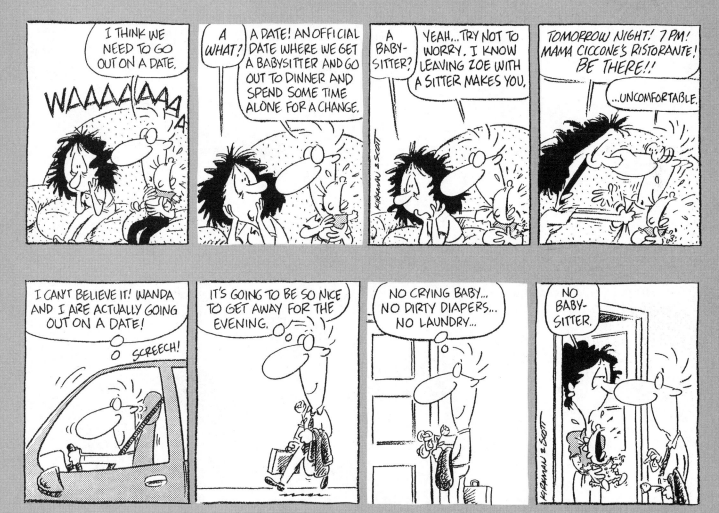

16

YOUR SHRIMP LOOKS GOOD...
MAY I HAVE A BITE?

SURE.

?

18

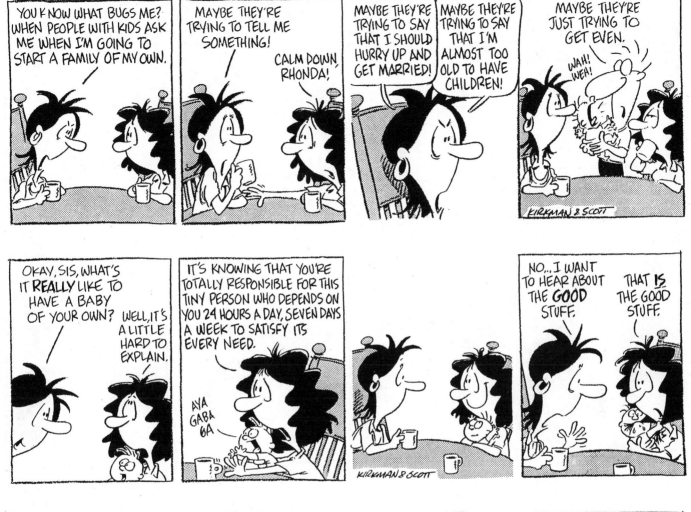

24

BABY BLUES®

RICK KIRKMAN BY JERRY SCOTT

LIVING IN A BABY-PROOFED HOUSE CAUSES WANDA TO OCCASIONALLY STEAL AWAY TO SPEND TIME WITH SOMETHING BREAKABLE.

KIRKMAN & SCOTT

32

BABY BLUES

BY RICK KIRKMAN / JERRY SCOTT

34

BABY BLUES®

RICK KIRKMAN / JERRY SCOTT BY

WHAT A CUTE LITTLE BOY!

GIRL.

CUTE KID... WHAT'S HIS NAME?

ZOE. IT'S A GIRL.

WHAT A GORGEOUS BABY! HE'S GOING TO BREAK A LOT OF HEARTS!

SHE!!...SHE'S GOING TO BREAK A LOT OF HEARTS!

PINK SEQUINS?

IT'S A LONG STORY.

37

41

BABY BLUES®

BY RICK KIRKMAN / JERRY SCOTT

GRANDCHILD O' MINE!

SUNG TO THE TUNE OF JERRY LEE LEWIS' "GREAT BALLS OF FIRE"

YOU FRAY MY NERVES
BUT I NEVER COMPLAIN.
I GOT MORE LOVE
THAN VARICOSE VEINS.
OH, WHAT A THRILL!
YOU'RE SUCH A PILL!
GOODNESS GRACIOUS!
GRANDCHILD O' MINE!

WE'LL PLAY ALL DAY
TILL MY HAIR LOOKS FUNNY,
YOU SMILE AT ME
AND YOU SWOON ME, HONEY!
IT'S YOUR NAPTIME—
I MUST RECLINE.
GOODNESS GRACIOUS!
GRANDCHILD O' MINE!

KISS ME, BABY!
OOOO-MMM! FEELS **GOOD!**
HUG ME BABY!
WELLLL, I SPOIL YOU ROTTEN
LIKE A GRANDMA SHOULD!
YOU'RE CRYIN'... I'M BUYIN'!
ANYTHING TO STOP
ALL THAT WHINE-
WHINE-
WHINE-IN'!

YOUR SCREAMS ARE LOUDER
THAN A HAND GRENADE,
DON'T NEED A BATTERY
IN MY HEARING AID.
A TANTRUM'S NEAR—
WE'RE OUTTA HERE!
GOODNESS GRACIOUS!
GRANDCHILD O' MINE!

WITH APOLOGIES TO HAMMER & BLACKWELL & JERRY LEE

44

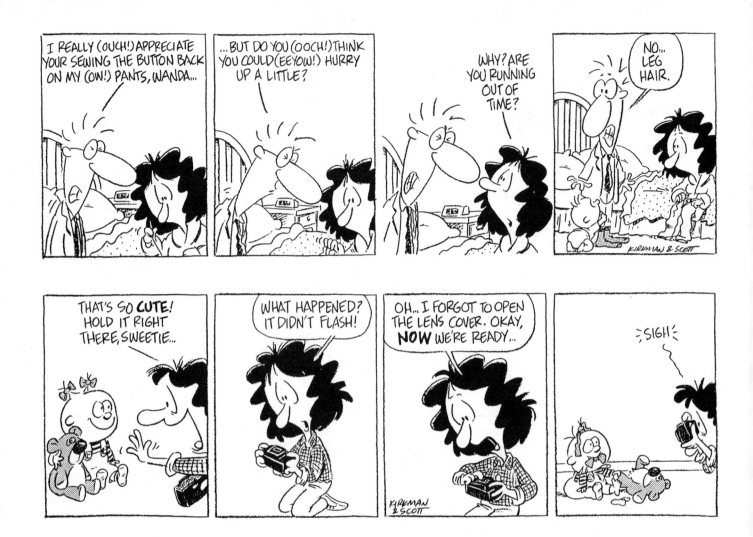

47

BABY BLUES

BY RICK KIRKMAN / JERRY SCOTT

32 FEET, 4 INCHES OF UNINTERRUPTED DROOL. IT'S A NEW RECORD!

EEYEEWW!

50

BABY BLUES®

RICK KIRKMAN / JERRY SCOTT BY

HOW DID YOUR DAY GO?

WELL, THAT 8 O'CLOCK CONFERENCE CALL WAS CANCELLED BECAUSE THEIR COMPUTERS WERE DOWN AND THEY COULDN'T GET TO THE INFORMATION WE...

AND THEN WE FOUND OUT THAT ALL THE MANUALS WE SENT OUT HAD EVERY OTHER PAGE UPSIDE-DOWN SO THEY WERE

SHHHHHH!

THAT'S BETTER.

SO ANYWAY, STAN CAME OVER AFTER HE FINALLY GOT THE FIGURES WE NEEDED, AND WE HAD

52

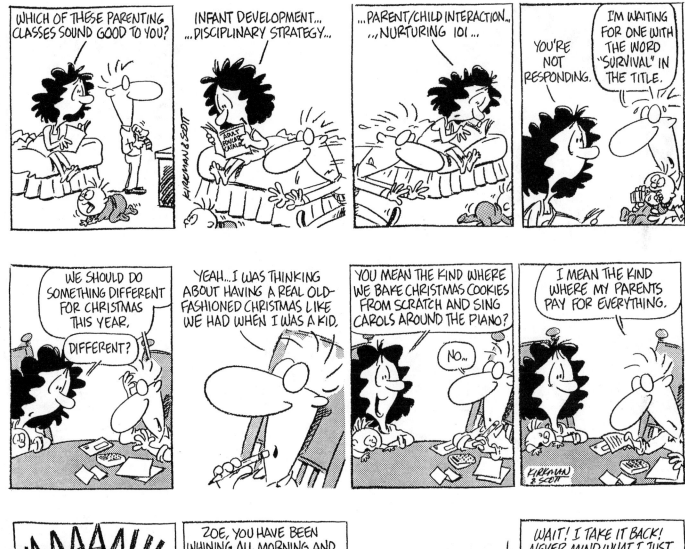

Panel 1: IT'S SO WEIRD SITTING HERE WATCHING MY SISTER PLAYING WITH **HER** DAUGHTER.

WHERE'S ZOE'S TICKLE BUTTON?

A-YA HAHA! KEEGEEGEE!

Panel 2: REALLY SWEET... IT ALMOST MAKES ME WANT TO HAVE A BABY...

Panel 3: ...TO **SIT**! YEAH! THAT'S IT! IT ALMOST MAKES ME WANT A BABY **TO SIT**!

Panel 4: WHOA! THAT WAS A CLOSE ONE, WASN'T IT?

MY STUPID BIOLOGICAL CLOCK MUST BE RUNNING FAST AGAIN.

Panel 5: ACCORDING TO THIS, AT AROUND TEN MONTHS, BABIES START GETTING INTO SOME **REAL** MISCHIEF.

YOU & BABY

Panel 6: LUCKY FOR US, ZOE IS ONLY EIGHT MONTHS OLD.

Panel 7: WHACK!

Panel 8: I THINK SHE MAY BE GIFTED.

Panel 9: HI, MOM, WHAT'S NEW?

OH, NOTHING.

Panel 10: I WAS JUST SITTING HERE THINKING ABOUT CUDDLING MY GRANDDAUGHTER.

Panel 11: I'M PRACTICING SO I'LL BE READY FOR HER AT CHRISTMAS.

THAT'S GREAT, MOM. I CAN'T WAIT.

Panel 12: WHAT'S YOUR MOM DOING?

ROCKING AIR BABIES.

BABY BLUES®
BY RICK KIRKMAN / JERRY SCOTT

71

LIVING ROOM ARCHAEOLOGY

Panel 1:
WHERE ARE YOU GOING TO PUT US ALL, DEAR?

MAC AND PAULINE WILL BE IN ZOE'S ROOM, YOU AND DADDY IN OUR ROOM AND DARRYL AND I WILL SLEEP ON THE FOLD-OUT COUCH.

Panel 2:
OH, HONEY, ARE YOU SURE? WE DON'T WANT TO PUT YOU OUT OF YOUR OWN BED...

NO! IT'S OKAY, WE INSIST.

Panel 3:
THE FOLD-OUT COUCH HAS AN EXCEPTIONAL MATTRESS!

Panel 4:
"EXCEPTIONAL MATTRESS." I GUESS THAT'S ONE WAY OF PUTTING IT.

CLAM UP. IT'S ONLY FOR A COUPLE OF WEEKS.

KIRKMAN & SCOTT

Panel 5:
THERE'S GRANDMA'S DARLING ENJOYING A COOKIE...

REC

Panel 6:
...AND THERE SHE IS CRAWLING AWAY...

REC

Panel 7:
THIS IS THE **NEWEST** DEVELOPMENT— STANDING UP!

REC

Panel 8:
AND THERE'S DADDY. WAVE, DADDY!

THE GRAMCAM

KIRKMAN & SCOTT

Panel 9:
PAULINE! LOOK AT THIS! ZOE IS CHEWING ON HER DOLL'S FOOT!

Panel 10:
KISS PAT SMOOCH! KISS!
KISS! PAT KISS! HUG KISS!
KISS SMOOCH HUG SMOOCH
PAT KISS KISS
PAT

Panel 11:
ZOE! WHAT HAPPENED TO **YOU**?

GRANNYLUST.

KIRKMAN & SCOTT

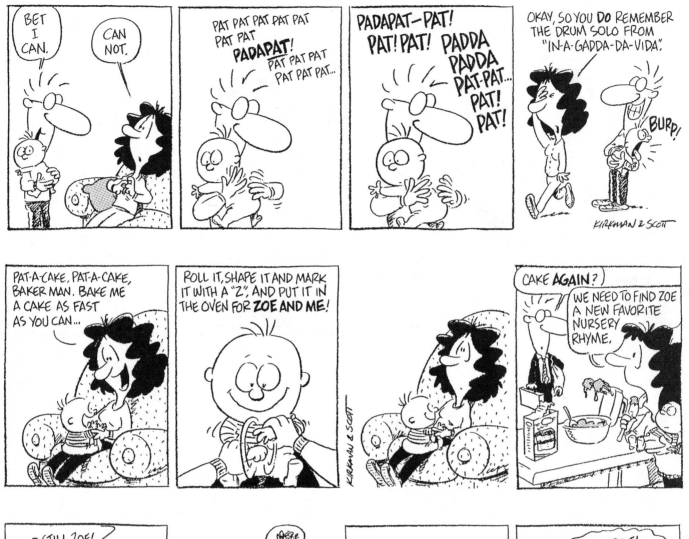

85

Panel 1: OKAY, DARRYL, LET'S SAY THAT YOU **DO** GET LAID OFF... WHAT WOULD WE DO ABOUT HEALTH INSURANCE?
GOOD QUESTION.

Panel 2: JUST TO BE SAFE, I'LL GO ASK STAN IF HE KNOWS HOW MUCH IT WOULD COST TO BUY IT ON OUR OWN... HANG ON.

Panel 3: PEEK-A-BOO!

Panel 4: WELL?
LET'S JUST SAY I WAS SURPRISED.

Panel 5: I'VE BEEN THINKING...LET'S SUPPOSE THAT YOU DO GET LAID OFF, MAYBE IT **WOULDN'T** BE THE END OF THE WORLD.

Panel 6: MAYBE IT WOULD BE AN OPPORTUNITY FOR YOU TO CHANGE CAREERS... TO BE SOMETHING THAT YOU'VE ALWAYS WANTED TO BE!

Panel 7: WHAT IS IT THAT YOU'VE ALWAYS WANTED TO BE?
A COWBOY.

Panel 8: OKAY, MAYBE IT **WOULD** BE THE END OF THE WORLD...

KIRKMAN & SCOTT

Panel 9: COME ON, ZOE... HAND THE BALL TO MOMMY!

Panel 10: HAND IT TO MOMMY! HAND IT TO MOMMY! HAND IT TO MOMMY! HAND IT TO MOMMY! HAND IT TO MOMMY! HAND IT TO MOMMY! HAND IT TO MOMMY! HAND IT TO MOMMY! HAND IT TO MOMMY! HAND IT TO MOMMY! HAND IT TO MOMMY! HAND IT TO MOMMY!

Panel 11: SHE UNDERSTOOD ME!
PLOP!

KIRKMAN & SCOTT

Panel 1:
WHAT ARE YOU DOING?

JUST PLAYING WITH SOME FIGURES.

KIRKMAN & SCOTT

Panel 2:
LET'S SAY I **DO** GET LAID OFF... IF WE'RE CAREFUL, I THINK WE CAN PAY ALL OF OUR BILLS **AND** HAVE ENOUGH MONEY TO LIVE ON WHILE I GO JOB HUNTING.

Panel 3:
REALLY?? THAT'S GREAT!

...PROVIDING THAT SOMEBODY HIRES ME WITHIN THE FIRST FORTY-FIVE MINUTES OR SO.

Panel 4:
HOW ARE THINGS AT WORK TODAY?

GRIM.

Panel 5:
EVERYBODY IS ON PINS AND NEEDLES WONDERING IF THEY'RE GOING TO BE THE NEXT ONE TO BE LAID OFF.

KIRKMAN & SCOTT

Panel 6:
I TELL YOU, IT'S A BATTLEFIELD IN HERE.

Panel 7:
RIGHT, LARRY?

HALT! WHO GOES THERE?

Panel 8:
WHERE'S STEVE?

LAID OFF. YESTERDAY.

STEVE? MY OLD BUDDY, STEVE??

Panel 9:
OH, STEVE! STEVE! STEVE!

SOB! SOB!

Panel 10:
...BETTER YOU THAN ME.

KIRKMAN & SCOTT

BABY BLUES

RICK KIRKMAN / JERRY SCOTT

UTILITIES...EIGHTY BUCKS. CAR PAYMENT... A HUNDRED AND SIXTY BUCKS...

WAAAA!

CREDIT CARD...SIXTY-FIVE BUCKS. INSURANCE... FIFTY-TWO BUCKS...

WAAAA

CABLE TV...TWENTY-FIVE BUCKS, CAR REPAIR...EIGHTY BUCKS. PEDIATRICIAN... NINETY-THREE BUCKS...

WAAAA

SIGH

WAAAAAA

YOU KNOW YOU'RE A PARENT WHEN YOU HAVE MORE DISPOSABLE DIAPERS THAN DISPOSABLE INCOME.

KIRKMAN & SCOTT

95

BABY BLUES®

RICK KIRKMAN / JERRY SCOTT

BABY BLUES®

RICK KIRKMAN / BY JERRY SCOTT

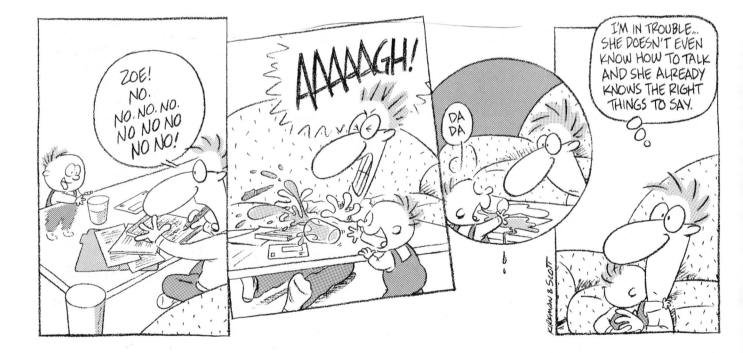

108

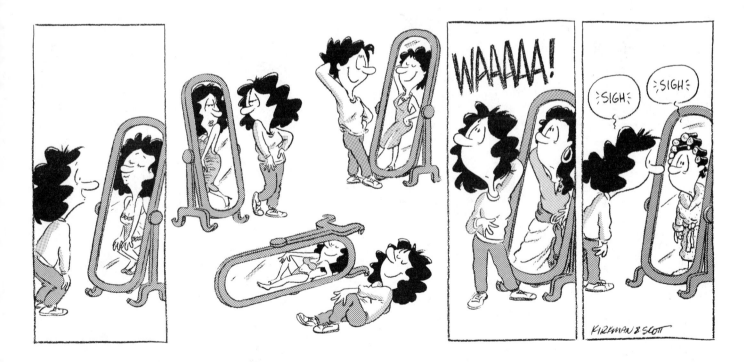

BABY BLUES

RICK KIRKMAN / JERRY SCOTT

PEEK-A-BOO!

—EE-BOO!

KIRKMAN & SCOTT

PEEK-A-BOO... THE ORIGINAL NON-PRESCRIPTION ANTI-DEPRESSANT.

RING!
RING!

MacPHERSON PLAYGROUND... MONKEY BARS SPEAKING...

KIRKMAN & SCOTT

IT'S AMAZING.

WHAT?

WABBA? WABBA? EEPOO

WHEN YOU LOOK AT YOUR OWN BABY YOU SEE SO MANY THINGS.

HOPE... FUTURE... INNOCENCE...

LAUNDRY... DIRTY DISHES... CHAOS...

IT MAKES MY HEAD SWIM.

IT MAKES MY BACK HURT.

EEEE!

KIRKMAN & SCOTT

OH, THINGS ARE GOING FINE, MOM.

IN FACT, WE HAD ENOUGH MONEY LEFT OVER THIS MONTH TO PUT A FEW DOLLARS INTO ZOE'S EDUCATION FUND.

THAT'S GREAT, HONEY!

YOU AND DARRYL ARE WISE TO START SAVING NOW... SHE'LL BE READY FOR COLLEGE BEFORE YOU KNOW IT!

COLLEGE? GET REAL MOM... THIS IS FOR PRESCHOOL!

KIRKMAN & SCOTT

121

THE END